MAPS OF DESIRE

Manuel Forcano
Maps of Desire

Translated from Catalan
and introduced by
Anna Crowe

Published by Arc Publications,
Nanholme Mill, Shaw Wood Road
Todmorden OL14 6DA, UK
www.arcpublications.co.uk

Original poems copyright © 2019, Manuel Forcano
Translation copyright © 2019, Anna Crowe
Introduction copyright © 2019, Anna Crowe
Copyright in the present edition © Arc Publications, 2019

978 1911469 79 7 (pbk)
978 1911469 80 3 (hbk)

Design by Tony Ward
Printed in Great Britain by T.J. International Ltd,
Padstow, Cornwall

Cover picture:
'The River Nile' by Xavier Puigmarti
by kind permission fo the artist.

ACKNOWLEDGEMENTS
The publishers wish to thank the editors of the following
magazines in which some of these poems have appeared:
Structo Magazine, *The High Window*, *Fras*, and *Asymptote*.

This book is in copyright. Subject to statutory exception and
to provision of relevant collective licensing agreements, no
reproduction of any part of this book may take place without
the written permission of Arc Publications.

This work was translated with the help of a grant
provided by the Institut Ramon Llull

Arc Publications 'Translations' series
Series Editor: Jean Boase-Beier

CONTENTS

Translator's Preface / 7

from
El tren de Bagdad / The Baghdad Train

20 / El tren de Bagdad • The Baghdad Train / 21
52 / Beirut • Beirut / 53

from
Estàtues sense cap / Headless Statues

60 / A la biblioteca • At the Library / 61
62 / Ibn Tulun • Ibn Tulun / 63
64 / Llengües • Languages / 65
66 / Monofisisme • Monophysitism / 67
68 / Taverna • Tavern / 69
70 / Escac mat • Checkmate / 71
72 / Una cosa mínima basta • The Slightest Thing Is Enough / 73
74 / Poema • Poem / 75
76 / Mística • Mysticism / 77
78 / Quantes vegades • How Many Times / 79
80 / A tres hores del Caire • Three Hours from Cairo / 81
82 / El riu immens • The Huge River / 83
84 / Misteris egipcis • Egyptian Mysteries / 85
86 / Segons el mapa • According to the Map / 87
88 / La casa de la felicitat • The House of Happiness / 89
90 / A la platja • At the Beach / 91
92 / A l'aeroport • At the Airport / 93
94 / Saurí • Seer / 95
96 / Per amor • For Love / 97
98 / Imatges • Images / 99

from
LLEI D'ESTRANGERIA / LAW GOVERNING ALIENS

102 / Nou món • New World / 103
104 / Cataclisme • Cataclysm / 105
106 / Istanbul • Istanbul / 107
108 / Les palmeres d'Al-Faium • The Palm Trees of Al-Fayoum / 109
110 / Museu egipci • Egyptian Museum / 111

from
CIÈNCIA EXACTA / EXACT SCIENCE

114 / No ets tu • It Isn't You / 115
116 / Passo el temps • I Spend My Time / 117
118 / Aquella llum • That Light / 119
120 / Època clàssica • The Classical Age / 121
122 / En aquell bar • In That Bar / 123
124 / Passo la nit • I Spend the Night / 125
126 / Com pluja erràtica • Like Passing Showers / 127
128 / El poema • The Poem / 129

Biographical Notes / 131

TRANSLATOR'S PREFACE

Manuel Forcano (born Barcelona, 1968) appears in the collection, *Six Catalan Poets* published by Arc in 2013. The book's editor, Pere Ballart, describes Forcano as a poet who has always been known for his "evocative lyrics, full of delicacy and sensibility." A Hebrew scholar and former academic, Forcano received his doctorate in Semitic Philology from the University of Barcelona, where he taught Hebrew, Aramaic and History of the Ancient Near East. He has taken part in the EU Manumed Project (2000-2004), cataloguing for libraries the Arab and Syrian manuscripts from countries on the southern shore of the Mediterranean, working in Aleppo and Damascus. He is the author of nine collections of poetry, and has translated works by Yehuda Amichai, Pinkhas Sadé, Ronny Someck, Amos Oz, Ibn Battuta, Marco Polo and E. M. Forster. He has received many literary awards, among them the Carles Riba Prize, the Jocs Florals de Barcelona prize, the Crítica Serra d'Or, and the International European Giovanni Tívoli Prize. He is a former Director of the Ramon Llull Institute.

This book draws on Manuel Forcano's four most recent collections – *El Tren de Bagdad* (The Baghdad Train), *Llei d'estrangeria* (Law governing aliens), *Estàtues sense cap* (Headless Statues) and *Ciència exacta* (Exact Science). When discussing the choice of a title, Manuel was very clear that the word *desire* had to be part of it, and I believe *Maps of Desire* succeeds in suggesting both the physical and psychological reaching-out towards other parts of the world that characterises the poems within its pages. These poems embrace the cities and landscapes and people of the Middle East, and the poet – a great traveller – uses geographical and historical references to deepen and inform the narrative, and also to lay before the reader the idea of the continuity, through many centuries, of human love and desire. The beauty, joy, grief and tenderness in these poems are universal and belong to every kind of human affection; no wonder, then, that Pere Ballart writes that Manuel Forcano has been described as "our foremost love-poet". No surprise, either, given the harmonious cadences and subtle rhythms of his writing, to learn that he is a gifted musician who has worked for Jordi Savall at the International Foundation Centre for Ancient Music in Barcelona.

The importance of memory is a theme that runs through Forcano's work, and in an extraordinary image in 'Poem' (p. 75), the poet reprimands himself for having lost touch with a former love, and for thinking that memory is something slight:

> And how little the memory weighs,
> as when in the Cairo metro
> we realise that between certain stops
> there flows above us
> the mighty Nile.

Memories can also be bitter, as in poems like 'Istanbul' (p. 107), or 'It Isn't You' (p. 115), where the poet ends by giving himself some sensible advice:

> Let none of this disturb you.
> It's like the clothing you wear every day:
> it has your shape
> but it isn't you.

The past has a way of repeating itself, of jogging the memory, that brings the reader up short with a shock. In 'The Baghdad Train' (p. 21), the narrative poem of over 400 lines at the beginning of the book, the poet tells us:

> From time to time everything grows confused
> as in that war-torn Syria
> described by Ammianus Marcellinus in his *Histories*

and into that brief gap after 'Syria' and before the next line there flashes before us the recent memory of the war-torn

Syria of our own century, and we are in two periods at once, aware of the griefs and atrocities endlessly recurring. With the countries of the Middle East composing the backdrop for most of these poems, the image of the desert features as a palimpsest that history writes on again and again, and which holds the remains of the past buried beneath its sands, sometimes buried forever by earthquake.

'The Baghdad Train' has as an epigraph a couplet by Ahmad Hassim:

> *What's left to us in this world that fades and darkens*
> *is the pleasure of remembering.*

That darkness is carried on in the opening lines where the poet is travelling on a train of the Barcelona metro, and describes himself as 'passing through the dark tunnel of your desire', where the jolting of the train will transport him back in memory to the train journey years before from Aleppo to Baghdad, travelling third class:

> hours of travel deciding whether or not to lick
> an unmoving drop of sweat
> so close to you that you are a tree
> rooted in that, the only water.

Images of thirst / desire and water / plenitude abound, and can be regarded as one of the tropes necessary in binding a long poem together, like the repeated refrain, 'That it doesn't rain in the desert is a lie.' It is love, the poet suggests, that opens up moments of illumination, bringing colour and definition, in which jouissance is suggested with great delicacy and beauty:

> with a caress, a landscape
> that is a monotone of nothingness bursts
> suddenly into the green of orchards with water tanks,
> and from the topmost blossom on the palm tree
> you see how the white ibis takes off.

There remains a pleasing ambiguity over where exactly this moment of illumination takes place: is the poet perhaps on the topmost blossom on the palm tree along with the white ibis? Love and desire, the poet reveals, have the ability to let you live in the moment, live in the present and enlarge and extend it infinitely. In Catalan, the word for 'water tank' is 'aljub', which is from the Arabic, 'al-jubb', meaning 'the well', and love is like water hidden beneath the sand:

> if you listen carefully,
> under the sand you can hear the water rising
> towards the roots of the palm trees,
> towards the wells, towards the chafe of bodies

Forcano's imagery is intensely visual, and in this poem about a journey taken in tremendous heat he finds endless ways of suggesting desire and pleasure through the image of water:

> and inside the carriage you saw mirages:
> a boy drinking from a bottle. What thirst
> makes us believe the other to be water?

Later on in *Maps of Desire*, in his poem 'Seer' (p. 95), he will describe fulfilment in an arresting image: 'Arms around the one I love, / I'm a dowser who has found water / and throws away his rods.'

His images of pleasure and homoerotic fulfilment are open, generous and free, rooted in landscape and experience, as in these lines from 'The Baghdad Train': 'Pleasure above all: a water-wheel / emptying its many scoops over you'; or again, 'Thirst for pleasures: / with one tug of the pulley the bucket penetrates / the well.' This playfulness is to be found throughout his work. In his poem, 'Beirut' (p. 53), the poet counters the devastation he sees in the war-damaged city with comic images for the lovers' desire:

> the rails on a track want
> the trains' metal wheels to fit exactly,
> the diving-suit desires the diver's head.
> We said this with our hands.
> And happiness,
> a donkey that has learned the knack
> of making the saddle-bags fall off.

In the 'Tavern' (p. 69) which 'looks like an ancient slave-market / from the time of the Mamluks', the customers are bewildered by the array of beautiful young men, and are described, in a mischievous but complex reversal of the power dynamic, as 'not knowing how to choose. / Like a fish / confronted by an array of fish-hooks.' In 'Mysticism' (p. 77) a lover reads out lines from the thirteenth-century Sufi mystic and poet, Ibn al-Farid, and later the poet smiles as he realises 'how many memories you owe / to mysticism.' In similarly humorous vein, 'Egyptian Mysteries' (p. 85), the title of a ten-volume book by Jamblic, the third century 'theurgist, a fanatic, a credulous philosopher and exegete', is a poem in which the poet's lover's lengthy disquisition is interrupted when 'all at once the city's thousand minarets / began to sing. / … / For what happened just afterwards. / I don't know which I should thank: whether philosophy / or religion.'

Forcano gives prominence to moments of seeing, as in 'you see how the white ibis takes off'; and 'inside the carriage you saw mirages'. In 'The Baghdad Train', eyes, like the image of water, become a useful trope, suggesting illumination, recognition, and understanding, but the converse can also be true:

> Patience is pretty – the Arabs say.
> The landscape was a blindman gazing into a mirror:
> a nothingness made of so much light,
> a waterless sea as flat as a ceiling.

And it is an image of eyes that do not see that predominates in the account of the sandstorm that lashes the train:

> The wind roaring in at the windows
> lashed us with sand:
> with eyes shut
> we travelled through the empire of light.
> A carriage of blind men
> under a metallic sun.

Often, the inner eye of memory guards its pleasures jealously, and refuses to let us locate them in the physical world, as the poet reminds us in poems like 'According to the Map' (p. 87), where he says, 'I don't recognise the house, / and I gaze at these façades / like one who searches the night sky / and doesn't know how to recognise / a single star.'

Images of division and separation pervade Forcano's work, and on the long journey of 'The Baghdad Train' the poet lays many examples before us: 'The track was the parting drawn through that bald landscape', he writes, and later on, 'But all at once the bridge over the Euphrates: / what eye wept that river / that cut the thirst of the desert into two banks?' Bridges come to be both physical and metaphorical, as when the train approaches the city of Deir-ez-Zor, where 'the banks are in love and the bridges are the kisses'.

The train itself becomes a powerful image of human solidarity, bringing moments of unity and communion, as when the passengers rejoice in the exquisite sights and scents of the date-forest they pass through, or when 'the water-seller served date-juice / in a single cup for the thirst of all'. In many poems, it is the incompleteness of the individual, the need of the other in order to become a whole, that is foregrounded: in 'Monophysitism' (p. 67), his friend wishes to explain to him 'the mystery of monophysitism: / whether Christ had a single nature, or two.' The lovers resolve this in their own way in lines of great beauty and tenderness:

> ... among the sheets
> the books that define monophysitism:
> two natures, one melted inside the other.
> How humble and exuberant all at once
> Paradise can come to be:
> in that narrow room
> the spread wings of so many angels.

In 'At the Library' (p. 61), with that lovely image of the other's breath 'like a silken flag / wafting over my face', and where the image of Babel lies just below the surface, the poet concludes that 'There are some things / with no precise meaning, / untranslatable. / ... / we are always just one half.' The inadequacy of language, paradoxically for this wonderful poet, is an idea that he clearly subscribes to, since it is frequently an instrument of separation; in 'Languages' (p. 65), which could equally well be translated as 'Tongues' – this is where the English language's wealth of near-synonyms becomes a disadvantage, and Catalan's smaller vocabulary makes for richness of ambiguity – Forcano tackles the subject head-on:

> We didn't speak the same language,
> a question of accent or dialect,
> but we spoke words to each other
> much as a painter populates with birds
> the sky of a painting.

After a sensuous list of the impressions of the day which came between them, the poet and his friend go back to 'smiling at each other between the words / that we didn't understand. //' and he concludes, 'How useless languages are: / desire knows how to say it all.'

Manuel Forcano is a scholar who wears his learning

lightly. Throughout 'The Baghdad Train', for example, there are passages where he pauses to tell us something about the places he is travelling through or passing, and the past events of history are transformed and illuminated, all contributing to the workings and dynamic of desire down the ages. Seeing the distant silhouette of the castle of Rahab, the poet recounts how 'In the eleventh century the Abassid prince Ibn Tauk / built it tall and powerful, he said, / as the waist of a lover.' The prince held feasts, and the 'cries of joy / that came from the banqueting hall / made the windows swell, grow round.' A sudden earthquake destroyed the castle and all within, but even now, Forcano writes, people 'search among the stones / for pieces of those mirrors where joy / remained engraved.' This surreal image shows very clearly this poet's consummate skill in expressing the enduring force of desire and the human need for love, and he will also employ paradox to convey this. In 'Images' (p. 99), Manuel Forcano quotes St John of Damascus who castigates iconoclasts and who wrote, 'What a book is for those who can read, / an image is for those who do not read.' Forcano is remembering an old love, and concludes mischievously,

> All I have left of you now is images.
> Images of pleasure. I shut my eyes
> to see them better.
> Those of you who can read
> will understand me.

And his poem, 'New world', whose imagery revisits the voyages of discovery, ends with two striking paradoxes where the reversal in terms of large and small and active and passive is daring and eloquent:

> Earth yearns so much
> for watchful eyes to see it.

Love is a port
that finally comes to a ship.

The poet's difficulty in writing about painful subjects is movingly expressed in a tiny poem near the end of the book, 'I Spend My Time' (p. 117), which speaks for all who attempt to write and to write honestly. I would like to conclude this introduction to *Maps of Desire* by quoting it in full, and by looking briefly at some of the nuts and bolts of translation:

I spend my time searching for words
and waste it among silences.
But they're there, between the fear of speaking
and the pain of staying silent,
stones that try to float
in a muddy swamp.

Anyone seeing this sight
will roar with laughter:
my ears are deafened
by the blank page in front of me.

Here is the original Catalan:

PASSO EL TEMPS

Passo el temps cercant paraules
i el perdo entre silencis.
Però són allà, entre la por de dir
i la pena de callar,
pedres que intenten surar
en una fanguera.

Algú pla que riurà
davant aquest espectacle:
se m'eixorden les orelles
davant el paper en blanc.

The poem in Catalan uses alliteration, mostly the letter 'p', and there are patterns of assonance, too, around syllables like 'er' and 'ar' and 'or', and patterns of short 'a' sounds too. In the English I have tried to find equivalent patterns, such as 'searching for words', and vowel sounds as in 'between the fear of speaking', 'waste / … / pain … staying', and 'stones … float', and alliterative patterns of words beginning with 's', 'st' or 'w'. In this way – and this is true throughout the book – I hope to suggest something of the musicality and sheer beauty of the sounds of the Catalan in Manuel Forcano's poetry. It has been a delight and a privilege to translate work of this high order, and I would like to express my gratitude to the editors of Arc Publications for asking me to carry out the task.

Anna Crowe

*Now I can say: I'm at the spring and drinking,
drinking until I die
of thirst from wanting more not knowing what
for this is how you do not truly die at all:
we live through lacking
something all the time.*

Joan Vinyoli

from
EL TREN DE BAGDAD / THE BAGHDAD TRAIN
(2004)

EL TREN DE BAGDAD

Ens queda el plaer de la memòria
en aquest món que s'apaga i s'enfosqueix.
                                        ÀHMAD HASSIM

Fa estona que corres per sota terra
travessant el túnel fosc del teu desig,
i el sotragueig suau del metro
et porta al cos d'hivern que tens
l'estiu i la calor de roba oberta
d'aquell viatge amb el tren de Bagdad
que va sortir impuntual i ple a vessar
de l'estació central d'Alep,
a Síria. Tercera classe:
vagons sense portes,
finestres sense vidres, seients de ferro,
camperols, soldats, gel·labes i turbants,
robes malgirbades, brunor d'or als colls,
braços, mans, veus, peus
descalços, tots fills d'Apol·lo,
diries. Amuntegament,
calors, molt poc espai:
hores de trajecte decidint si llepar o no
una gota de suor quieta
tan a prop teu que eres un arbre
arrelat en aquella única aigua.
Als lavabos dels vagons atrotinats,
sexe entre l'òxid i el mirall esquerdat.
Les rodes arrancaven guspires
als rails. "Perquè he vingut
a afegir-te'm a la set"
–va dir-te desajuntats els llavis.
L'amor és també una mena de velocitat:
amb la carícia, un paisatge
monòton de no-res esclata
de sobte en el verd d'hortes amb aljubs,

THE BAGHDAD TRAIN

> *What's left to us in this world that fades and darkens*
> *is the pleasure of remembering.*
> AHMAD HASSIM

For some time you've been travelling underground
passing through the dark tunnel of your desire,
and the gentle jolting of the metro
brings you, brings to that winter body of yours,
the summer and the heat of loose clothing
of that journey on the Baghdad train
that pulled out late and full to bursting
from Aleppo's Central Station,
Syria. Third class:
carriages without doors,
windows without glass, iron seats,
country people, soldiers, djellabas and turbans,
dishevelled garments, golden tan on necks,
arms, hands, voices, bare
feet, each one a son of Apollo,
you'd say. A great piling-up,
heat and more heat, very little room:
hours of travel deciding whether or not to lick
an unmoving drop of sweat
so close to you that you are a tree
rooted in that, the only water.
In the toilets of the damaged carriages
sex between the rust and the cracked mirror.
The wheels were snatching sighs
from the rails. "Because I've come
to fasten you to myself in thirst,"
he told you, when your mouths parted.
Love is also a kind of speed:
with a caress, a landscape
that is a monotone of nothingness bursts
suddenly into the green of orchards with water tanks,

i al cim de la flor de la palmera
veus com arrenca l'ibis blanc el vol.

La via era la clenxa d'aquell paisatge calb:
el desert és un excés de buit,
un tros de cel caigut a l'inrevés
com un insecte que agonitza panxa enlaire.
Diuen que no té ni camins ni direccions,
que tot és esgarriar-se, però tots anem
segurs
cap als miratges: aigua imaginada
que crepita lluny com fusta seca
al fons d'aquest espai que no t'hi cap a la mirada.
Però és prou ample, per fi,
per a tots els besos no donats,
per a totes les carícies projectades en els cossos
que no t'ha ofert l'atzar,
per a tot el desig-llavor mai no arrodonit en fruita.
Els remolins d'aire estripaven la superfície del desert
igual que fan al mar
les aletes dels taurons.
El vent roent per les finestres
ficava sorra a fuetades:
travessàvem d'ulls clucs l'imperi de la llum.
Sota un sol metàl·lic
un vagó de cecs.

Arribàvem a la ciutat d'ar-Raqqa,
parada dels camellers de la ruta de Palmira
i on diuen que els poetes enamoraven els califes.
A l'estació, vestit a la turca i fes al cap,
l'aiguador servia aigua de dàtils
en un únic got per a la set de tots:

and from the topmost blossom on the palm tree
you see how the white ibis takes off.

The track was the parting drawn through that bald landscape:
the desert is an excess of emptiness,
a chunk of sky fallen upside down
like an insect dying, belly to the air.
They say that it has no roads, no directions,
that it's all a going astray, but we all go
confidently
towards the mirages: imagined water
that crackles in the distance like dry wood
at the back of this space you can't see when you look at it.
But it's spacious enough, in the end,
for all the kisses not given,
for all the caresses projected on to the bodies
that chance has not offered you,
for all the seeds of desire never swollen into fruits.
The whirlwinds of air ripped the surface of the desert
just as they do at sea,
ripping the fins of sharks.
The wind roaring in at the windows
lashed us with sand:
with eyes shut
we travelled through the empire of light.
A carriage of blind men
under a metallic sun.

We were coming to the city of Raqqa,
a camel-drivers' stop on the road to Palmyra
and where they say the poets made the caliphs fall in love.
At the station, dressed in Turkish fashion with a fez on his head,
the water-seller served date-juice
in a single cup for the thirst of all:

llàgrimes de palmera
per alegrar els colls secs –deia.
Un venedor m'oferí essència de flors,
mirra, aigües de gesmil, almesc,
olis de mareselva dels oasis,
pol·len perfumat, i en una ampolla,
neu del Líban.
S'ungia mans i braços i me'ls feia olorar:
quanta primavera pot suportar un cos?
Un noi repicava uns gots de vidre als dits de cada mà
i per demostrar que no es trencaven
en va llançar un amb força a terra:
"Intacte!" – cridava, i me l'oferia.

Desert endins,
el sostre del túnel que travessàvem era el sol,
una cintura descordada de llum líquida,
una paret que queia damunt nostre
sense acabar mai d'esclafar-nos.
Però de sobte el pont sobre l'Eufrates:
quin ull plorava aquell riu
que partia la set del desert en dues ribes?
del plaer de quin déu naixia?
quina llum paria sense dolor aquell blau?
I vas enfonsar-hi els ulls
per gaudir com les pedres nues
al fons de la carícia de l'aigua
en la quietud i aquell silenci
entre la placidesa de les algues,
banderes de la lentitud.
Car de vegades tot se't fa confús
com en aquella Síria en guerra
descrita per Ammià Marcel·lí en les Històries:
en tu també cremen castells,

tears from the palm tree
to make dry throats happy – he kept saying.
Another offered me essence of flowers,
myrrh, jasmine-water, musk,
oil of honeysuckle from the oases,
scented pollen, and in a bottle,
snow from Lebanon.
He anointed hands and arms and made me smell them:
how much spring can a body bear?
A boy was jingling glass cups on the fingers of both hands
and to show that they were unbreakable
dashed one of them with great force on the ground:
"Intact!" he cried, offering me one.

Far into the desert,
the ceiling of the tunnel we were going through was the sun,
a shameless belt of liquid light,
a wall falling down on top of us
that would never finish crushing us.
But all at once the bridge over the Euphrates:
what eye wept that river
that cut the thirst of the desert into two banks?
From which god's pleasure was it born?
What light painlessly gave birth to that blue?
And you sank your eyes in it
to rejoice like the naked stones
in the depths of the water's caressing
in the quietness and that silence
among the calm of the waterweeds,
those flags of slowness.
For from time to time everything grows confused
as in that war-torn Syria
described by Ammianus Marcellinus in his *Histories*:
in you too castles burn,

s'enfonsen naus i moren príncepts.
Se t'extravien mortes de set
les tropes. En cap ciutat
no et sents segur i els camins
són vies entre camps d'arbres talats.
Demanes asil a qui, com tu,
ho ha perdut tot,
i des d'una finestra veus surar,
Eufrates avall, un cos inert
amb una sageta clavada al mig del pit.
L'amor que tenies.

Vam fer entrada a la ciutat de Deir ez-Zor:
s'estimen les ribes i els ponts són els petons.
Allà és tortura no complir el desig
i el riu fa cada cop més meandres
perquè no troba el mar. Mig nus,
nois color de fusta i cabells negres
saltaven de cap des del pont dels Francesos
i s'enfonsaven suaus a l'aigua
com fan les peülles dels camells
en la sorra de les dunes.
Alguns saltadors arrossegaven el pit pel fons
amb moviments lents entre bombolles,
i de plaer
el riu floria escumes.

A la soc de Deir ez-Zor
els beduïns oferien crancs del riu
i peixos en paneres: "Tot sense espines!",
cridava amb veu forta un dels venedors,
i recolzava les mans brunes
al gel.
El vent feia voleiar als caps de les beduïnes

ships sink and princes die.
Your troops wander astray,
die of thirst. In no city
do you feel safe and the roads
are paths between fields of felled trees.
You ask for shelter from one who, like you,
has lost everything,
and from a window you watch a lifeless
body float down the Euphrates
with an arrow stuck in the middle of its breast.
The lover you once had.

We came into the city of Deir ez-Zor:
the banks are in love and the bridges are the kisses.
There it is torture not to fulfil desire
and the river makes even more meanders
because it cannot find the sea. Half naked,
black-haired boys the colour of wood
were diving head-first from Frenchmen's bridge
and smoothly entering the water
just like the camels' hooves
in the sand of the dunes.
Some of the divers drew their breast along the riverbed
in slow movements among bubbles
and for sheer pleasure
the river flowered in foam.

In the Deir ez-Zor souk
bedouin were offering crayfish
and fish in baskets: "All free of bones!"
one of the vendors was calling in a loud voice
and resting his brown hands
on the ice.
The wind set the coloured kerchiefs fluttering

els mocadors de colors com abans els estendards
en les antigues reunions dels clans:
de nit al desert feien un foc
i competien a veure qui deia en vers
els mots que més eren com les flames.
El silenci era un escorpí a l'aguait
sota una pedra. La pluja
oferia a beure els seus mugrons.
Que no plou al desert és mentida:
si escoltes bé,
sota l'arena sents emergir l'aigua
cap a les arrels de les palmeres,
cap als pous, cap al frec dels cossos
i els gemecs rere les tendes i a les cledes
on descansen d'ulls insomnes
els camells.

Avançava el tren
per aquell paisatge desèrtic d'ull de cec,
només ça i lla un tamariu raquític,
arbustos amb flors sense color,
espines amb arrels.
I de sobte, al lluny,
la silueta del castell de Ràhab:
al segle IX el príncep abbàssida Ibn Taük
va construir-lo alt i poderós – va dir –
com la cintura de l'amant.
Mantenia el dia encès tota la nit
amb festes sumptuoses: torxes,
miralls, coixins de seda, i als tambors
mans d'esclaus númides, odalisques
amb vels i llentioles,
fruita en safates d'or i argent,
copes bolcades i rialles,

on the heads of the Bedouin like the banners
at the old meetings of the tribes:
at night in the desert they lit a fire
and competed to see who could say in lines of poetry
the words that were most like the flames.
The silence was a scorpion lying in wait
beneath a stone. The rain
offered up its nipples to drink from.
That it doesn't rain in the desert is a lie:
if you listen carefully,
under the sand you can hear the water rising
towards the roots of the palm trees,
towards the wells, towards the chafe of bodies
and the groans behind the tents and in the pens
where the camels with their sleepless eyes
are resting.

The train was moving on
through that desert landscape like a blindman's eye,
with only here and there a rickety tamarisk,
bushes with colourless flowers,
spines with roots.
And then suddenly, far-off,
the silhouette of the castle of Rahab:
In the eleventh century the Abassid prince Ibn Tauk
built it *tall and powerful*, he said,
as the waist of a lover.
He kept the day on fire all night long
with sumptuous feasts: torches,
mirrors, silken cushions, and on the drums
the hands of Numidian slaves, odaliscs
with veils and sequins,
fruit on gold and silver trays,
overturned cups and laughter,

cossos com raïms que una mà esprem.
Que no plou al desert
és mentida. Els crits de goig
que sortien de la sala de banquets
feien més rodones les finestres.
A fora ploraven d'enveja els guardians
que patrullaven pels merlets.
De cop, un terratrèmol.
Cap crit. I el silenci
i el mateix núvol de pols d'ara
suspès damunt les runes.
Hom cerca entre les pedres
bocins d'aquells miralls on va quedar gravat
el goig. Encara ara
somniem el plaer dels altres.

Era un os tot escurat aquell desert
i el riu hi fluïa trist i en silenci
com per a un sord una boca en moviment.
A l'altra riba s'estenien imponents
les muralles derruïdes de la ciutat de Dura Europos:
la gran Torre 19 mig tombada
com un arbre amb les arrels malaltes.
L'any 256 els perses invasors
hi irrompien cavant una obertura.
Els romans havien anat a trobar-los sota el túnel.
S'enfrontaren a mans nues en l'obscuritat
i es reconeixien en palpar-se:
amb rostre rasurat: romans,
amb barba: perses.
Però una part de la torre va esfondrar-se al seu damunt
i els arqueòlegs han trobat els esquelets dels enemics
abraçats sota la runa. És el gest més perfecte
l'abraçada.

bodies like grapes that a hand presses.
That it doesn't rain in the desert
is a lie. The cries of joy
that came from the banqueting hall
made the windows swell, grow round.
Outside, the guards on sentry-duty
up on the ramparts wept for envy.
Suddenly, an earthquake.
Not a cry. And the silence
and the same cloud of dust as now
suspended above the ruins.
People search among the stones
for pieces of those mirrors where joy
remained engraved. Even now
we dream the pleasure of others.

It was a scoured bone, that desert,
and the river flowed there, sad and silent
as a speaking mouth would be for a deaf man.
Stretching away imposingly on the other bank
were the tumbled walls of the city of Dura Europos:
the huge Tower 19 half-listing
like a tree with sickly roots.
In 256 the invading Persians
broke through by digging a breach.
The Romans had gone to meet them down in the tunnel.
Their bare hands confronted each other in the dark
and they recognised each other by touching:
with shaven face: Romans;
with beard: Persians.
But part of the tower collapsed on top of them
and archaeologists found skeletons of these enemies
clasped in each other's arms beneath the ruins. The embrace
is the most perfect of gestures.

De nit feia un sol negre.
El cel era el cos poderós d'un esclau
que dorm després d'una jornada sota els fuets.
I al vagó, entre els embalums,
un braç en la fosca va argollar-me:
vàrem fer el breu camí
de la roba descordada a la nuesa.
Que poc espai de llavis
entre els besos. Que ràpid
el foc. Que suau
la cendra. A fora,
resplendien lluny en la negror
les flames altes de les refineries
com reflexos d'una cadena d'or
damunt un tors pelut.
El tren travessava el túnel de la nit
fins que et vas desvetllar a l'alba:
el dia, espelma nova,
naixia per cremar. El cel
tenia un color de cames nues
i encara et veieres rastres de les carícies a la pell
talment la senda que deixen les caravanes
per les dunes.

El tren va fer parada a Abú Kamal:
als guals per on ara els ramats passen el riu
al segle III els parts van fer presoner Valerià,
l'emperador de Roma:
fugia espantat de l'enemic. L'exèrcit,
a la desbandada. Amb els seus guardes
va refugiar-se en un bosc alt de canyissos.
Per fi un moment de pau,
un descans per al vell emperador:
descavalcar, treure's el casc,

At night it was as black as it could be.
The sky was the powerful body of a slave
who sleeps after a day beneath the lash.
And in the carriage, amid the encumbrances,
an arm in the darkness wrapped itself round me:
we took the quickest way
of unfastened clothing to nakedness.
What little space for lips
among the kisses. How swift
the blaze. How soft
the ashes. Outside,
shining far off in the blackness
were the lofty flames of the refineries
like reflections of a golden chain
on a shaggy torso.
The train travelled through the tunnel of night
until you woke up with the dawn:
day, like a new candle,
was being born in order to burn. The sky
was the colour of naked legs
and still you might see traces of caresses on skin
just like the track the caravans leave
on the dunes.

The train halted at Abu Kamal:
at the fords where now the flocks cross the river,
in the third century the Parthians took Valerianus,
emperor of Rome, prisoner:
he was fleeing in terror from the enemy. The army
in total disarray. With his guards
he hid in a bed of tall reeds.
At last a moment of peace,
a rest for the old emperor:
to dismount, take off his helmet,

posar els peus a l'aigua, mig adormir-se
a l'ombra dels plomalls. Els corsers
tancaven els ulls en abeurar-se.
Però un escamot de parts
va irrompre a crits entre les canyes,
i segrestaren l'ancià,
que va veure com els seus darrers soldats
queien morts tombant els joncs en flor.
S'enduia el corrent pètals i sang.
Arribaven lentes al fons del riu
les espases lluents.
I s'emportaren Valerià desert endins
encadenat,
el paladar esquerdat de set,
les dents del sol clavades al seu cos.
El seu fill Galià, a Roma,
es posava al cap la diadema
i amb un brindis somrient
acceptava les genuflexions de tots.
No el blasmeu: tot tipus d'afectes
pateixen desercions.

La paciència és bonica –diuen els àrabs.
El paisatge era un cec contemplant-se en un mirall:
no res de tanta llum,
un mar sense aigua pla com un sostre.
Cremava l'esquelet de ferro del vagó
i de l'alta temperatura se't rebentava de suor
la pell. Feixuc vernís
que t'imposava la quietud
i t'enfonsava els ossos a la sang.
Totes les sivelles obertes. Els botons
fora dels traus. L'abric de la nuesa.
I dins mateix del vagó veies miratges:

bathe his feet in the water, doze a little
in the shade of the plumed reeds.
Their chargers closed their eyes as they drank.
But a troop of Parthians rode yelling into the reeds,
and took the old man prisoner,
who saw how the last of his soldiers
fell dead, causing the flowering reeds to bend.
The current bore away petals and blood.
The shining swords
came slowly to rest at the bottom of the river.
And they carried off Valerianus into the desert
and in chains,
his palate split with thirst,
the sun's teeth fastened in his flesh.
In Rome, his son Galianus
placed the diadem on his own head
and with a smiling toast
accepted the genuflections of all.
Do not curse him: all kinds of affections
suffer desertions.

Patience is pretty – the Arabs say.
The landscape was a blindman gazing into a mirror:
a nothingness made of so much light,
a waterless sea as flat as a ceiling.
The iron skeleton of the carriage burned
and the high temperature made your skin drip
with sweat. A slow glaze
that imposed stillness on you
and pushed your bones deep into your blood.
Every buckle undone. Buttons
loosed from buttonholes. Nudity's coat.
And inside the carriage you saw mirages:

un noi bevia d'una ampolla. Quina set
ens fa creure l'altre aigua?
Tots els somnis
són un oasi al fons de l'horitzó,
un jardí d'ombres, sentir-te
blat al cos i una mà que pessiga suau
la punta de les espigues.
I sobretot el plaer: una sínia
buidant els seus catúfols damunt teu.
Que no plou al desert és mentida.

I de sobte al vagó, una remor,
batibull i aglomeració a les finestres,
dits assenyalant lluny un punt de verd
que creixia a mesura que avançàvem:
palmades i rialles, l'alegria
i exclamacions de joia:
"Déu és bell i per això li agrada la bellesa"
– va recitar algú de l'Alcorà.
Ens acostàvem als palmerars d'as-Sawari,
una selva immensa de palmeres
nascudes dels pinyols de dàtils
escurats a dos durant un bes
en les cites secretes dels beduïns
les nits nues de lluna.
Despullar-se
com es desfulla a la pèrgola
la vinya. Set de plaers:
d'un cop de corriola penetra la galleda
el pou.

Deixant enrere el gep sec del desert,
de sobte va engolir-nos
un túnel de nou milions d'arbres de palma.

a boy drinking from a bottle. What thirst
makes us believe the other to be water?
All dreams
are an oasis far out on the horizon,
a garden of shadows, feeling like wheat
in your body and a hand gently squeezing
the tips of the ears.
Pleasure, above all: a water-wheel
emptying its many scoops over you.
That it never rains in the desert is a lie.

And suddenly in the carriage a murmur,
jostling and crowding at the windows,
fingers pointing at a far-off line of green
that grew as we travelled onwards:
clapping and laughter, happiness
and exclamations of joy:
"God is beautiful and that is why he delights in beauty,"
someone recited from the Qur'an.
We were approaching the palm-groves of as-Sawari,
an immense forest of palm trees
risen from the spat-out stones
scoured by couples during a kiss
in the secret rendez-vous of the Bedouin
on nights when there was no moon.
Undressing
the way the vine lets fall its leaves
on the trellis. Thirst for pleasures:
with one tug of the pulley the bucket penetrates
the well.

Leaving the dry hump of the desert behind,
we were suddenly swallowed
by a tunnel of nine million palms.

El tren corria per l'entreombra
d'aquell verger immens i turgent.
Era el temps de la collita
i els dàtils d'un negre brillant
o voluptuosament vermells
suaven sucre.
Us ha plogut mai mel damunt?
Uns homes penjaven dels troncs,
es gronxaven entre les fulles
i amb falç d'or lluents al sol
feien caure els ramells.
Els camperols cantaven:
Què és l'amor
que ens fa veure més altes les palmeres?
La mel se'ls enganxava als músculs
i fulguraven com quan el sol
il·lumina l'interior d'una magrana,
ungits
com reis o guerrers antics
a punt per la batalla.
Van saludar el tren amb crits, rialles,
i feien equilibris abraçats a les palmeres,
ocells entre els cabells dels arbres.

A Salihiyya va pujar al tren
un encantador de serps:
la melodia d'una flauta va despertar
el rèptil d'escates brillants i coll inflat.
Pel plaer d'aquella música la serp s'alçava a poc a poc
i es recargolava com a les boques
les llengües en un bes.
La bellesa és perillosa
i t'hipnotitza el verí del que t'atreu:
goses,

The train ran through the half-shade
of that immense and swollen orchard.
It was harvest time
and the dates, black and glistening
or a voluptuous red,
sweated sweetness.
Have you ever been rained on by honey?
Men were hanging from tree trunks,
they swayed among the fronds
each with a gold sickle, and shining in the sun
they caused the bunches to fall to the ground.
The harvesters sang:
What is love
that makes the palms seem ever taller?
The honey stuck to their muscles
and they glowed as when the sun
lights up the inside of a pomegranate,
anointed
like kings or ancient warriors
about to join battle.
They greeted the train with shouts, laughter,
and swung, clinging to the palms,
birds amongst the hair of the trees.

Boarding the train at Salihiyya
a snake-charmer:
the melody of a flute awoke
the reptile with its brilliant scales and engorged neck.
For the pleasure of that music the snake rose up slowly,
and coiled itself as tongues do
when mouths meet in a kiss.
Beauty is dangerous
and the poison that draws you hypnotizes you:
like the flute-player's hand,

com la mà estesa del flautista
davant els ullals fins de la serp,
temptar la teva sort.
Tu també has estat valent:
has besat com fruita que mossegava boques,
no t'ha fet por abandonar-te al goig
amb qui has trobat més exacte al teu desig
i has fet teu el risc de l'arbre fràgil
que vol sencera
l'esquena de l'ós gratant-se al tronc.
Es va fer silenci al vagó
quan el flautista va callar:
la serp va caure de cop
a la cistella.

Vam arribar a la ciutat d'ar-Ramadi.
Durant el sultanat d'Abú Saïd
– diuen les velles cròniques –
una tempesta la va colgar de sorra
i només el crostó del minaret
va sobreviure. S'enfosquí el cel
com els ulls coberts de l'ase
que dóna voltes al molí,
fins que va alçar-se en espiral la ira del vent
i tots van descobrir que la sorra mossega,
que és mar que s'alimenta de naufragis:
immens derelicte la ciutat
sota l'arena. Un llaüt sense cordes
va dir el silenci de després.
Tot va quedar aplanat
com un llit fet.

Però van reconstruir la vila: nous carrers
damunt el vol encallat d'uns ànecs dins les dunes,

stretched out before the snake's slender fangs,
you dare
to tempt your fate.
You too have been courageous:
you have kissed like a fruit that bites mouths,
you weren't afraid to abandon yourself to joy
with one whom you found best fitted your desire
and you made your own the risk of the delicate tree
that the bear's back wants all to itself
as it rubs itself against the trunk.
Silence fell in the carriage
when the flute player stopped playing:
the snake dropped suddenly
into the basket.

We came to the city of Ramadi.
During the sultanate of Abu Saïd –
so say the chronicles –
a storm buried it in sand
and only the tip of the minaret
survived. The sky grew dark
as the blinkered eyes of the ass
that keeps the mill turning,
until the wrath of the wind rose spiralling upwards
and everyone discovered that sand can bite,
that it's a sea that feeds on wreckage:
immense and derelict the city
beneath the sand. An unstrung lute,
said the silence afterwards.
Everything remained as smooth
as a just-made bed.

But they rebuilt the town: new streets
above the grounded flight of a few ducks within the dunes,

noves palmeres crescudes
de pinyols al clot de les boques
dels cadàvers. Nous pous d'on,
de tant en tant,
emergeixen crits en l'aigua.
A ar-Ramadi cal caminar
talment damunt d'un llac congelat:
amb por de l'esberla,
atents al fons.

Va entrar lentament el tren a l'estació
com una nau de vela que sense vent
travessa una badia.
Onades de gent van atansar-se
i tot de mans per les finestres
ens oferien de bat a bat obertes
síndries i peixos del canal,
bresques de mel, plats de llegums,
estores perses, figuretes
dels antics déus mesopotàmics,
albercocs, prunes, retrats
del rei Faisal,
i una pluja desendreçada de paraules.

Que no plou al desert
és mentida. I un noi que venia despertadors
va preguntar-me: "quina hora en punt
serà la nostra?" El desig
és una mena de fractura
com d'una primavera flors pintades
o algú corrent nu sobre la neu,
urgent,
com a la mà d'un nadó
un ganivet. Però el tren

new palm trees grown
from date stones in the hole of corpses' mouths.
New wells out of which,
from time to time,
cries would rise up through the water.
At Ramadi you have to walk
as though across a frozen lake:
for fear of shattering what's there,
mindful of what's below.

The train pulled slowly into the station
much as a sailing ship with no wind
crosses a bay.
Wave after wave of people came close
and all with their hands through the windows
offered us watermelons split-open
and fish from the canal,
honeycomb, vegetable dishes,
woven Persian rugs, figurines
of the old Mesopotamian gods,
apricots, plums, portraits
of King Faisal,
and a disorderly shower of words.

That it never rains in the desert
is a lie. And a boy selling alarm-clocks
asked me: "When exactly
will it be our time?" Desire
is a kind of fracture
like spring flowers painted,
or someone running naked across the snow,
urgent,
like a knife in the hand
of a newborn baby. But the train

va arrencar de nou i em va deixar
amb migpartida una resposta.
Els venedors
van perseguir els vagons
atropellant-se, cridant preus,
i enarborant cal·ligrafies
com els tres mil genets omeies
que en la batalla de Saffín l'any 657
duien fulls de l'Alcorà clavats a les puntes de les llances.
Però el tren era més ràpid
que els seus camells de guerra
i vas fugir sense que cap de llurs sagetes
fes diana en tu. Perdies sang,
però.

Si el rellotge de sorra es trenca,
perd el temps per la cintura estreta
i el gest senzill de ser
s'acaba. Com quan la sequera
escanya els aiguamolls
i els peixos moren atrapats
en tolls cada vegada més petits.
En la llum de la tarda el tren travessava
una generosa zona de conreus:
aigua somrient per les canals
i jo reposava els ulls
en la vastitud dels arrossars en flor,
en les barraques construïdes als marjals,
en les ales blanques de les garses,
en la pell fosca dels búfals,
quan emergien lents del fang.
Aigua poada per a la set
aquest paisatge.
Veta d'or aquests records.

started again and left me
with my reply cut in half.
The vendors
pursued the carriages,
jostling each other, calling out prices,
waving calligraphies
like the three thousand Umayyad horsemen
who in the battle of Siffin in 657
bore pages of the Qur'an stuck on the points of their lances.
But the train was swifter
than their war-camels
and you fled without any of their arrows
finding its mark in you. And yet
you bled.

If the hourglass shatters,
it loses time through its narrow waist
and the simple expression of being
ends. As happens when drought
chokes the marshes
and the fish die trapped
in ever shrinking pools.
In the afternoon light the train passed through
a generous area of cultivation:
water smiled along the channels
and I rested my eyes
on the vastness of rice fields in flower,
on the huts built beside the marshes,
on the white wings of herons,
on the dark hide of the buffaloes
as they climbed slowly out of the mud.
Well-water drawn for thirst,
this landscape.
A vein of gold, these memories.

I ara t'hi arribes com un miner
amb la llum al casc. És ric
qui somriu en recordar.

D'una nuesa us diria
imagineu arenes. O el tacte a la boca
dels tramussos. Car et queda al paladar
el regust de bes als racons més amagats del cos.
Això pensava quan tot d'una
m'avisaren que ens acostàvem a Bagdad:
mira el Tigris
gaudint del sol vertical que l'assassina
com un heretge que riu dins la foguera.
Tanta llum per il·luminar el desordre
de l'emoció de l'arribada:
Bagdad, ciutat dels somnis.
I volies fer com els beduïns que, des del desert,
s'agenollen agraïts
en distingir les seves grans muralles,
la majestat dels seus palaus,
els mil minarets que canten,
les barques amb veles de colors,
la multitud als ponts,
les fonts que t'inviten a la set,
els jardins d'un temps que passa
sense despullar les roses
a la llum d'un sol que daura:
és mentida que al desert
no plou.

I per fi el teu vagó
va travessar el gran arc de triomf de l'estació:
cridòria a les andanes,
sirenes, fums, banderes,

And now you come to them like a miner
with a light on his helmet. You're rich
if you smile while remembering.

Of a naked body I would say to you
imagine sand dunes. Or the touch of lupins
on the mouth. For on your palate there remains
the taste of a kiss on the most hidden corners of the body.
I was thinking that when all at once
I was told we were approaching Baghdad.
Look at the Tigris
rejoicing in the sun vertically overhead that murders it,
like a heretic laughing in the fire.
So much light to illuminate the disorder
of the excitement of arrival:
Baghdad, city of dreams.
And you wanted to do as the Bedouin do who, from the desert,
kneel down in gratitude
as they make out its great walls,
the majesty of its palaces,
the thousand minarets that are singing,
the boats with their coloured sails,
the crowds on the bridges,
the fountains that invite your thirst,
the gardens of time that is passing
without plucking the roses
in the light of a sun that spills gold:
it's a lie that in the desert
it doesn't rain.

And at last your carriage
has passed the station's great triumphal arch:
uproar on the platforms,
klaxons, smoke, flags,

i el xiscle de les rodes que frenaven.
Un cor petit d'ocell
pot desplegar ales immenses:
els altres paisatges de la teva vida
se't feien gerra esbucada,
neu desfeta, llit en flames.
Algú va invitar-te
a pujar al palanquí del seu camell:
si un mar vol banyar-te,
et quedaràs a la platja?
¿no volen les nanses de les tasses
dits a dins?

Però tot d'una despertes dins el metro.
Celebres content aquells records,
i et dius en veu alta: ja no cal més
envejar el passat dels altres.
Però t'equivoques com qui en un concert
aplaudeix de sobte quan no toca.
Per a tu,
igual que per als animals del zoo,
el temps és el transcórrer lent dels dies
que t'allunyen d'aquell passat a camp obert
on eres de cos
salvatge. Ja no saps
si tot allò fou o és autèntic:
¿és possible tancar a la memòria estreta
la velocitat dels músculs del guepard?
¿tanquen les sabates de ciutat que dus
les peülles de sàtir que tingueres?
I sents fer-se't a dins
els anells dels anys dels arbres
i cada cop t'enfonses més o peses menys:
viure és ser un vaixell

and the screech of the wheels, braking.
A bird's small heart
can shake out immense wings:
the other landscapes of your life
made you a hollow jug,
trampled snow, a bed in flames.
Someone invited you
to climb into the palanquin on his camel:
if a sea wants to bathe you,
will you stay on the beach?
Do cup-handles not want
fingers in them?

But suddenly you wake up on the metro.
You celebrate those memories happily,
and say to yourself aloud: you don't need
to envy other people their past any longer.
But you are mistaken, like someone at a concert
who suddenly applauds when they shouldn't.
For you,
as for animals at the zoo,
time is the slow elapsing of days
that take you from that past into open country
where you were wild
in body. You don't know now
whether all that was or is authentic:
is it possible to bind the speed of a cheetah's muscles
in narrow memory?
Can the city shoes you are wearing
enclose the satyr's hooves you wish you had?
And you feel being laid down inside you
the tree rings of the years
and each time you go in deeper or weigh less:
to live is to be a ship

que suporta el blau del cel al seu damunt
i a sota el blau del mar.

L'enyor és un peix que es contorsiona
al bec punxegut d'una grua.
Debades et poses a recer d'un foc
que ho ha de cremar tot:
ets la llenya del fred futur
d'uns altres. I surts del metro
i a peu per l'avinguda
d'aquesta nit d'hivern
tornes a casa, a la de sempre,
final del teu trajecte,
al teu barri de Vallcarca
de la ciutat on vius:
Bagdad.

that bears the blue of the sky above
and the blue of the sea below.

Longing is a fish writhing
in a crane's sharp beak.
You shelter in vain from a fire
that must consume everything:
you are the firewood of the future coldness
of others. And you come out of the metro
and walking along the avenue
of this winter night
you come back home, the one you've always had,
the end of your journey,
home to your district of Vallcarca
in the city where you live:
Baghdad.

BEIRUT

En algun lloc del cos amaguem l'odi.
A les mans que acaricien. Al tou dels llavis.
Als genolls dels qui es prosternen per pregar,
als dits dels qui se senyen.
I tota una ciutat hi cap
a l'ull d'un franctirador que apunta,
a l'ull buit d'una víctima.
El cel odiava els sostres i els terrats
i va enfonsar-los:
les finestres van vomitar la runa,
els soterranis van engolir la gent.
Només el mar es va salvar d'aquell naufragi.

Però reneix el blat segat
perquè no s'acaba mai la fam,
i ara reconstrueixen la ciutat
amb vista a les devastacions futures.
Talment la llum, que de dia
caurà en nit, i el record,
primer vigorós a la memòria
per després perdre el color
com una bandera massa temps al vent.
Bastides, grues, pedra,
i paletes fent ciment:
creixen a poc a poc els edificis
sense saber quan seran runa,
i els bladars maduren sense saber la falç
ni què vol dir ser pa
i que et masteguin.

"És ficar de braç nu la mà en un rusc,
la guerra. Les bombes,
una única nota en una partitura.
Les alarmes avisaven: doneu-vos els últims besos,

BEIRUT

Somewhere in the body we hide hatred.
In hands that caress. In the softness of lips.
In the knees of those who prostrate themselves to pray,
in the fingers of those who make the sign of the cross.
And an entire city fits
in the eye of a sniper as he takes aim,
in the vacant eye of a victim.
Heaven hated the roofs and terraces
and buried them:
the windows spewed out rubble,
cellars swallowed people up.
Only the sea was rescued from that shipwreck.

But the ruined wheat comes back
because there is no end to hunger,
and now they are rebuilding the city
with an eye to future devastations.
Just like light which from day
fades into night, and memory,
at first so sharp in the mind
then later leaching colour
like a flag too long in the wind.
Scaffolding, cranes, stone,
and bricklayers making cement:
the buildings slowly grow
not knowing they will be rubble,
and the wheat fields ripen never knowing the sickle
nor what it means to be bread
so you may be eaten.

"War means sticking your bare hand
into a hive. Bombs
are the single note in a musical score.
The sirens sound their warning: kiss for the last time,

i després dormir
amb la por que una caravana de formigues
se t'endugui." Així em vas explicar
aquells dies que ara corregies
com qui aixeca el cap de les flors
en un jardí després d'una tempesta.
"Arrenca'm –vas demanar-me–
les ortigues dels records.
L'incendi de la neu.
L'ofec al fons del mar
del blau." I vam caminar junts
tota la Línia Verda cap al mar
com un projectil que sap contra què l'han disparat.

"Tot és mesurable –deies.
Fins i tot la forma que deixen les onades
a les ribes. Geometria fractal:
l'impuls de l'aigua en càlculs i paràboles."
I jo era cada cop més a prop teu
com un vaixell que arriba
i se li va fent menys profund el mar.
L'escuma atrapada als esquelets de les petxines
el vent la feia tremolar. I els muetzins
no sabien cap a quina immensitat cantar:
al cel buit,
al mar ple de cel,
a la platja que anava a cada passa
descalça als nostres peus.

Els noms dels barris de Beirut
–Hamrà, Manara, Abú Rumane, Aixrafiye–
eren plens de marques de metralla a les façanes,
però la ciutat tenia aquells dies
el color dels ulls d'algú que els tanca,

and then fall asleep in the fear that a column of ants
may carry you off." This was how you described
to me those days that you are now repairing
like one who lifts up the heads of flowers after a storm.
"Pull out," you begged,
"the nettles of my memories.
The burning snow.
The drowning at the bottom of the sea
of blue." And together we walked
the entire length of the Green Line to the sea
like a missile that knows what it was fired at.

Everything can be measured – you were saying.
Even the shape left by the waves
on the shore. Fractal geometry:
water's thrust in parabolas and calculations.
And all the time I was getting closer to you
like a ship arriving
while the sea around it continues to grow less and less deep.
The foam caught on the skeletons of shells
trembled in the wind. And the muezzin
didn't know where, at which immensity, to direct their singing:
at the empty sky,
at the sea full of sky,
at the beach which lent itself to our feet
with every barefoot step.

The names of the districts of Beirut –
Hamrah, Manarah, Abu Rumaneh, Ashrafiyeh –
were covered in shrapnel marks on their façades,
but the city wore, for those days,
the colour of the eyes of someone who closes them,

tranquil,
per prendre el sol:
els rails d'una via volen exactes
les rodes metàl·liques dels trens,
l'escafandre desitja el cap del bus.
Ens ho vam dir amb les mans.
I l'alegria,
un ase que ha après el gest
de fer caure les alforges.

Però no és fàcil haver estat immensament feliç.
Les llimonades que vam prendre a la Corniche
ara ja han perdut aquell gust d'àcid i de mar
que de vegades també tenen els besos.
Els gaudis,
com retenir-los?
Sempre torna, incòmoda,
la set. És inútil el vol dels insectes
contra el vent.

La nit gira al voltant d'un far encès:
ressegueixo molts cops al mapa
l'itinerari de l'avió
per sobre el blau pintat del mar fins a Beirut.
I quan ara hi paro el dit damunt
em sembla reviure aquell estiu,
aquella cambra: tu i jo
en una guerra cos a cos
embolicats en la bandera blanca dels llençols.
Fruita que mossegava boques.
I per la finestra oberta
una llum que ja no pot ser més.
L'ombra del sol.

calmly
to take the sun:
the rails on a track want
the trains' metal wheels to fit exactly,
the diving-suit desires the diver's head.
We said this with our hands.
And happiness,
a donkey that has learned the knack
of making the saddle-bags fall off.

But it's not easy, having been immensely happy.
The lemonades we drank on the *corniche*
have now lost their flavour of sourness and sea
that kisses also sometimes share.
Pleasures,
how to hold on to them?
It always inconveniently comes back,
thirst. The flight of insects is powerless
against the wind.

Night circles around a flashing lighthouse:
I often trace once more on the map
the plane's itinerary
over the painted blue of the sea to Beirut.
And now when I rest my finger on it
I seem to relive that summer,
that room: you and I
at war, body to body
wrapped in the sheets' white flag.
Fruit biting our mouths.
And through the open window
a light that is not to be, any longer.
The shadow of the sun.

from
ESTÀTUES SENSE CAP / HEADLESS STATUES
(2013)

A LA BIBLIOTECA

*La saviesa dels romans rau al seu cervell,
la dels indis en llur fantasia, la dels grecs
en l'ànima, la dels àrabs en la llengua*

As-Saddiqi s. x

No dominaves el meu alfabet
ni jo l'accent del Delta del teu àrab,
però em vas veure estranger
i vas venir a demanar-me
que t'ajudés a cercar una paraula al diccionari.
Et vas acostar tant a mi,
el teu alè com una bandera de seda
onejant pel meu rostre.
Jo passava fulls i fulls,
endarrere i endavant,
dissimulant, fent temps
per no trobar mai aquell mot.
Fins que et vaig dir:
                      "Hi ha coses
sense un significat precís,
intraduïbles".
Però el dubte va quedar-se resolt:
som sempre una meitat.

AT THE LIBRARY

> *The wisdom of the Romans lies in their brain,*
> *that of the Indians in their imagination, that of the Greeks*
> *in the spirit, that of the Arabs in the language*
>
> As-Saddiqi (10th century)

You hadn't mastered my alphabet
nor I your Arabic with its accent of the Delta,
but you saw I was a foreigner
and came over to ask me
to help you search for a word in the dictionary.
You came up so close to me,
your breath like a silken flag
wafting over my face.
I turned over page after page,
forwards and backwards,
pretending, taking my time
so as not to find that word.
Until I told you:
                    There are some things
with no precise meaning,
untranslatable.
But the question was resolved:
we are always just one half.

IBN TULUN

Me n'adono mentre pujo l'escala de cargol
del minaret cilíndric de la mesquita d'Ibn Tulun:
duies tatuat al cos un laberint
del qual encara no he sabut sortir.
Cada cop que et repenso
erro el camí, la direcció,
i el mapa dels carrers del Caire no m'ajuda:
no hi apareixen les rues fosques del basar,
que eren les teves,
i on em vas ensenyar
com es regateja
quan desitges una cosa de debò.

Me n'adono mentre baixo l'escala de cargol
del minaret cilíndric de la mesquita d'Ibn Tulun:
a l'alt balcó sense barana dels records
la llum m'ha enlluernat.
I no he vist res sinó tu
des d'allà dalt.

IBN TULUN

It comes to me while climbing the spiral staircase
of the cylindrical minaret of the Ibn Tulun mosque:
tattooed on your body was a labyrinth
from which I haven't yet discovered how to escape.
Each time I think of you again
I mistake the path or the direction,
and the map showing all the streets of Cairo is no help:
it doesn't show the dark lanes of the bazaar,
which were yours,
and where you taught me
how to haggle
when you really want something.
It comes to me while making my way down the spiral staircase
of the cylindrical minaret of the Ibn Tulun mosque:
on memory's high balcony with no parapet
the light dazzled me.
And I could see nothing but you
from high up there.

LLENGÜES

No parlàvem la mateixa llengua,
qüestió d'accent o dialecte,
però ens dèiem paraules l'un a l'altre
com un pintor pobla d'ocells
el cel d'un quadre.
Mentre a xarrups preníem te
i a la ràdio sonava l'Um Kulzum,
ens explicàvem la canícula del dia,
l'espera impacient de trobar-nos,
les llums de colors i la música
a les barques sobre el Nil,
l'olor de les guaiabes,
dels dàtils rojos, l'infern de la nit
quan cadascú tornés a casa.
Hi havia gent que et saludava
i em presentaves, i jo responia
amb una fórmula educada,
el gest de la mà al pit,
i tornàvem a l'univers tranquil
d'acceptar tot el que no podíem expressar,
de somriure'ns entre els mots
que no enteníem.

Que inútils les llengües:
el desig ho sap dir tot.

LANGUAGES

We didn't speak the same language,
a question of accent or dialect,
but we spoke words to each other
much as a painter populates with birds
the sky of a painting.
While we sipped tea
and the *Um Kulzum* rang out on the radio,
we explained to each other how tedious the day had been,
waiting impatiently to meet,
the coloured lights and music
on those boats on the Nile,
in the bazaar the scent of the guavas,
of the red dates, the hell that was night
when each went to his own house.
There were people greeting you
and you introduced me, and I responded
with a polite formula,
the gesture of the hand on the breast,
and we went back to the calm universe
of accepting everything we couldn't express,
of smiling at each other between the words
that we didn't understand.

How useless languages are:
desire knows how to say it all.

MONOFISISME

Va ser a Shubra, un barri brut
i escrostonat del Caire. Casa teva
era petita, dues habitacions:
la cuina d'olor d'espècies,
i el catre d'olor teva.
Aquell capvespre volies mostrar-me
els llibres coptes,
el retrat del vell patriarca sobre el llit,
i explicar-me el misteri del monofisisme:
si Crist tenia una única naturalesa, o dues.
Les nostres, però,
es van encendre de desig
en un foc que no consum
com la bardissa ardent al Sinaí.
A la llum d'un únic fluorescent
vam contradir la regla dels pares del desert:
"Que cap home no agafi la mà del seu company
ni res més d'ell." I entre els llençols
els llibres que definien *monofisisme*:
dues naturaleses, l'una fosa dins de l'altra.
Que humil i exuberant alhora
pot arribar a ser el Paradís:
en aquella cambra estreta
les ales esteses de tants àngels.
I xiuxiujàvem com si fóssim davant les icones
i pregàvem que el temps,
que és del dimoni – vas dir –
no consumís
aquella nit.
        A trenc d'alba
et vaig deixar dormint.

MONOPHYSITISM

It was in Shubra, a filthy
and dilapidated quarter of Cairo. Your house
was small, two rooms:
the kitchen smelling of spices,
and the bed smelling of you.
That evening you wanted to show me
the Coptic books,
the portrait of the ancient patriarch over the bed,
and explain to me the mystery of monophysitism:
whether Christ had a single nature, or two.
Our own, however,
kindled with desire
in a fire that doesn't consume
like the burning bush on Sinai.
By the light of a single fluorescent bulb
we contradicted the ruling of the desert fathers:
"Let no man reach for the hand of his companion
nor anything else of his." And among the sheets
the books that define *monophysitism*:
two natures, one melted inside the other.
How humble and exuberant all at once
Paradise can come to be:
in that narrow room
the spread wings of so many angels.
And we whispered as though facing the ikons
and we prayed, that time,
which comes from the devil – you said –
might not consume
that night.
        At daybreak
I left you sleeping.

TAVERNA

Sembla un antic mercat d'esclaus
del temps dels mamelucs,
i fàcilment els reconeixes:
                            àrabs de ciutat,
pels cabells negres perfumats;
beduins del oasis,
pels seus collarets d'or;
negres de Núbia,
per tants anells als dits;
cristians de l'Alt Egipte,
per les creus tatuades als canells;
i, com tu, alguns estrangers
amb no prou alcohol
per tanta set.
I no saber triar.
Com un peix
davant molts hams.

TAVERN

It looks like an ancient slave market
from the time of the Mamluks,
and you easily recognise them:
                              city Arabs,
by their black and perfumed hair;
Bedouin from the oases,
by their gold necklaces;
black-skinned Nubians,
by the many rings on their fingers;
Christians from Upper Egypt,
by the crosses tattooed on their wrists;
and, like you, a few foreigners
with not enough alcohol
for so much thirst.

And not knowing how to choose.
Like a fish
confronted by an array of fish-hooks.

ESCAC MAT

Molts detalls de tu
i de nosaltres junts
s'han esborrat: passen els dies
com unes mans que ens han deixat d'acaronar.
Ja no sé ben bé qui eres
ni què vam dir-nos aquells vespres
entre el fum de tantes pipes d'aigua
als cafès a l'aire lliure:
m'embriagava veure't,
i jugar a escacs era una excusa
per contemplar els teus dits
movent les peces del teu exèrcit
cap a mi. Que dolces
poden arribar a ser de vegades
les derrotes: la teva torre
tombant sobre el tauler
el meu rei.
Moltes nits
vas aliniar davant meu
els teus peons.

CHECKMATE

Lots of things about you
and about us together
have faded: the days go by
like hands which have ceased their caressing.
I don't really know who you were, now,
nor what we used to tell each other those evenings
amid the smoke of so many bubbling hookahs
in the open-air cafés.
I got drunk just seeing you,
and playing chess was an excuse
for watching your fingers
moving the pieces of your army
towards me. How sweet
it can sometimes turn out to be,
being defeated: on the board
your castle knocking over
my king.
Many nights
you lined up your pawns
to face me.

UNA COSA MÍNIMA BASTA

No sé quin espai
ni quin protagonisme té el record
en el present de cada dia,
però una cosa mínima basta
per posar la memòria en moviment.
Per exemple, uns mitjons.

En venies damunt el capó d'un cotxe
a la plaça de l'estació central del tren
just als peus descalços de granit
de l'enorme estàtua de Ramsès II.
En un país de calor extrema
on tothom va amb babutxes o peu nu,
se't va fer evident per què jo te'n comprava cada dia:
somreies, i me'ls venies més barats,
de fil d'Escòcia, de llana australiana
o cotó egipci
pels freds que mai poguessin arribar…

I esperàvem el moment
del contacte
en tornar-me les monedes calentes del canvi
de la teva butxaca
al meu palmell.

THE SLIGHTEST THING IS ENOUGH

I don't know what space
or what role remembering occupies
in the present of each day,
but the slightest thing is enough
to jog the memory and set it going.
Some socks, for example.

You were selling them from the bonnet of a car
in the square beside the central railway station
right next to the bare granite feet
of the enormous statue of Ramses II.
In a country of extreme heat
where everyone wears slippers or goes barefoot,
it became obvious why I would buy some from you
every day:
you smiled, and sold them to me more cheaply,
made of Scottish linen, or wool from Australia
or Egyptian cotton
against the chills that couldn't ever occur…

And we'd wait for the moment
of contact
when you gave me the warm coins of my change
from your pocket
into my palm.

POEMA

No sé què se n'ha fet de tu.
T'he perdut el rastre com una obra antiga
de lectura ja impossible
i de la qual només sabem
el títol.

Com et desitjava,
fins que un dia vas venir a casa,
moneda que repica a la llauna
del captaire.

La robustesa d'un gran tronc
el plaer pot destralejar-la:
l'alegria de dos arbres caiguts
per un mateix tall d'acer
lluent.

I que lleuger el record,
com quan al metro del Caire
no ens adonem que entre algunes parades
flueix damunt nostre
el Nil immens.

Sí sé què se n'ha fet de tu:
poema.

POEM

I don't know what has become of you.
I have lost all trace of you like an ancient work
impossible now to read
and of which we know only
the title.

How I desired you,
until one day you came to the house,
a coin that rings
in the beggar's tin.

The strength of a great trunk
can be axed by pleasure:
the joy of two trees felled
by the same stroke
of shining steel.

And how little the memory weighs,
as when in the Cairo metro
we realise that between certain stops
there flows above us
the mighty Nile.
Yes I do know what has become of you:
poem.

MÍSTICA

Em va llegir uns versos d'Ibn al-Farid:
"Tot el meu cos el va besar amb totes les boques,
i en com em besava hi havia tots els besos".
I amb el llibre a la falda
i els dits entre les pàgines,
ens vam quedar en silenci.
A l'espera de viure-ho.
De provar-ho.

Ara somrius en descobrir
quants records deus
a la mística.

MYSTICISM

He read me a few lines by Ibn al-Farid:
"He kissed my whole body with all his mouths,
and in the way he kissed me were all the kisses there are."
And with the book in his lap
and his fingers between the pages,
we sat not speaking.
Waiting to live it.
To try it.

Now you smile as you discover
how many memories you owe
to mysticism.

QUANTES VEGADES

Quantes vegades en un museu
t'has identificat amb les antigues estàtues
sense cap.
          Un cop tu també el vas perdre
per algú de qui ara
no pots dir sinó aquell passeig pel Nil
amb barca i vela blanca: les palmeres
gairebé acaronaven la pell del riu, i allargant els braços
collíem dels joncs les flors de ploma. Estirats a coberta,
camisaoberts al sol, una mà lànguida a l'aigua,
un fil d'escuma als dits,
i el desig que emergia,
cocodril obrint la filera dels ullals.
Vam començar a fer broma i a esquitxar-nos
fins a quedar xops, perles d'aigua
a les rialles, els cabells, a la cara, al pit.
Es va barrejar a les copes
el vi i l'aigua del riu,
i ens ho vam beure.
Quantes vegades.

HOW MANY TIMES

How many times in a museum
have you identified with the ancient statues
that have no head.
                      Once you too lost yours
over someone about whom now
you can relate only that trip along the Nile
in a boat with a white sail: the palm trees
almost embraced the river's skin, and stretching out our arms
we plucked feathery flowers from the reeds. Lying in the shade,
shirts unbuttoned to the sun, a languid hand in the water,
fingers trailing a line of foam,
and desire surfacing,
a crocodile opening a row of eye-teeth.
We started to joke and splash each other
until we were soaked, beads of water
in our laughter, our hair, faces, breasts.
Mingling in our glasses
were wine and river water,
and we drank it.
How many times.

A TRES HORES DEL CAIRE

Tens Alexandria a tres hores del Caire.
Torna-hi. Podràs revisitar el fortí otomà,
contemplar els carreus de l'antic far a l'escullera,
passejar pels bells jardins
de la mesquita d'Abú Abbàs,
entaular-te als restaurants del port
i escurar amb les mans
el peix del dia.

Però bé saps
que no hi aniràs per res d'això.
Només tornaràs a aquell cafè
i seuràs a la mateixa taula al vespre.
Impacient, com qui espera
l'imminent canvi del semàfor,
vigilaràs la porta.
I resaràs perquè aparegui.
Fins que aparegui.

THREE HOURS FROM CAIRO

Three hours from Cairo you have Alexandria.
Go back there. You'll be able to revisit the small Ottoman fort,
admire the ashlar of the ancient lighthouse on the breakwater,
stroll through the beautiful gardens
of the Abu Abbas mosque,
sit at a table in one of the restaurants by the harbour
and pull apart with your hands
the catch of the day.

But you know quite well
that you'll go there for none of these things.
You will go back to that one café
and sit at that same table in the evening.
Impatiently, like someone waiting
for the traffic lights to change at any moment,
you'll keep your eyes on the door.
And you'll pray for him to appear.
Until he does appear.

EL RIU IMMENS

A molt més, no vam gosar.
La ciutat era, per a mi,
tota nova. Per a tu,
massa vella.

Van ser només uns dies.
Per a mi no prou llargs,
per a tu massa pocs.
Hi vam afegir les nits.

I el goig,
com una diana a la paret
plena de dards. Tu i jo,
forquilla i ganivet
al plat buit després de l'àpat.
Però sovint l'amor és provar de retenir aigua
amb els dits d'una mà oberta.

I, amb nosaltres, el riu immens:
fluint cap al mar, com jo,
sempre allà, com tu.

THE HUGE RIVER

For much more, we didn't dare ask.
The city for me,
was all new. For you,
too old.

They were only a few days.
For me not long enough,
for you too few.
We added on the nights.

And joy,
like a bull's eye on the wall
full of darts. You and I,
knife and fork
by the empty plate after the meal.
But often love means trying to hold water
in the fingers of an open hand.

And with us, the huge river:
flowing all the way to the sea, like me,
always there, like you.

MISTERIS EGIPCIS

Intentaves dir-me alguna cosa
i vas recórrer als *Misteris egipcis* de Jàmblic:

«… un teürg, un fanàtic, un crèdul, un filòsof i exegeta del segle III que en deu llibres va recollir les pràctiques endevinatòries i tots el rituals del món antic per a saber el futur. Descriu el rang dels éssers contemplats: des d'aquells amb poders catàrquics fins als que només resulten ser fantasmes o presències vanes i enganyoses. També tracta la naturalesa de les aparicions, l'impacte del diví i els desordres que sempre causa la bellesa, i exposa aleshores les dues classes d'èxtasi: quan els deus t'ocupen l'ànima, o quan hi fan brillar una llum. Jàmblic també es pregunta quina eficàcia tenen les pregàries, quin és el valor dels sacrificis, i encara uns capítols més enllà explica fil per randa com esperits i dimonis poden arribar a posseir-te, a enfollir-te. Així mateix parla dels planetes, dels eclipsis, dels horòscops, de la relació dels astres amb la fatalitat o amb la sort, per exemple, d'haver-nos trobat tu i jo aquesta tarda…».

Vas interrompre el teu discurs
perquè tot d'una els mil minarets de la ciutat
es posaren a cantar.

El que va passar just després
no sé a qui agrair-ho: a la filosofia
o a la religió.

EGYPTIAN MYSTERIES

You were trying to tell me something
and had recourse to Jamblic's *Egyptian Mysteries*:

"… a theurgist, a fanatic, a credulous philosopher
and exegete of the third century who in ten volumes
gathered together the divinatory practices and all the
rituals of the ancient world for predicting the future. He
describes the status of the beings he contemplates: from
those with cathartic powers to those who turn out to be
nothing more than phantasms or unreal and delusional
presences. He also deals with the nature of apparitions,
the impact of the divine and the disorders that beauty
always causes, and lays bare at the same time the two
kinds of ecstasy: when the gods occupy your soul, or
when they cause a light to shine there. Jamblic also asks
what efficacy prayers have, what is the value of making
sacrifices, and a few chapters further on he explains in
great detail how spirits and demons come to possess
you, make you go mad. And thus he goes on to speak of
planets, eclipses, horoscopes, of the relationship of the
stars with fate or with the good fortune, for example, of
having found each other, you and I this evening…".

What you were saying was interrupted
because all at once the city's thousand minarets
began to sing.

For what happened just afterwards
I don't know which I should thank: whether philosophy
or religion.

SEGONS EL MAPA

Segons el mapa era aquí.
O potser un o dos carrers més enllà.
Era aquesta porta, o bé
aquesta altra?...
En la memòria del goig
queden consignats altres detalls.

Aquelles nits, a altes hores,
a la teva cambra:
la llum d'una única bombeta
dibuixava les nostres ombres
sobre els pocs mobles,
fruita en un plat,
la roba descordada.

Segons el mapa era aquí.
Però ara, a la llum del dia,
al cap dels anys,
no reconec la casa,
i contemplo les façanes
com qui escruta un cel de nit
i no hi sap reconèixer
cap estrella.

El passat és un pou begut.

ACCORDING TO THE MAP

According to the map it was here.
Or possibly one or two streets farther on.
Was it this door, or maybe
this one?…
In pleasure's memory
other details are still recorded.

Those nights, in the small hours,
in your room:
the light from a single bulb
sketched our shadows
on scant furniture,
fruit on a plate,
scattered clothing.

According to the map it was here.
But now, in the light of day,
after all these years,
I don't recognise the house,
and I gaze at these façades
like one who searches the night sky
and doesn't know how to recognise
a single star.

The past is a well drunk dry.

LA CASA DE LA FELICITAT

No pensis mai que perds.
Serva com sigui el que ara saps
que excepcionalment
vas viure:
         van ser només
uns pocs dies d'estiu,
nits de matalàs a la terrassa,
esmorzars de te i galetes
al seu pis petit i humil
com una flor de gessamí,
just davant del palau ara barrat
del rei Faruk
de qui et va explicar l'abdicació forçada,
el seu exili, els seus festins opípars
com els nostres
de besos.   La data
del meu bitllet d'avió
ens va obligar a l'adéu :
abdicació forçada,
exili.

Ara ho has convertit tot en aquests versos
i cada cop que els rellegeixes
saps que vas habitar,
ni que fos per uns pocs dies,
la casa de la felicitat.

THE HOUSE OF HAPPINESS

Don't ever believe you're losing.
Let what you now know serve as example
of how remarkably
you lived:
         they were only
a few summer days,
nights with the mattress on the terrace,
breakfasts of tea and biscuits
in your flat, small and humble
as a jasmine flower,
right in front of the palace, now closed-off,
of King Farouk
whose forced abdication you explained,
his exile, his banquets sumptuous
as our own
of kisses.
         The date
on my plane ticket
compelled us to say goodbye:
forced abdication,
exile.

Now you have turned it all into these lines
and every time you read them again
you know you lived,
if only for a few days,
in the house of happiness.

A LA PLATJA

Pren el sol de braços oberts
sobre una tovallola de colors.
Els seus dits joguinegen
amb l'arena.
            Des d'on tu seus
veus el seu cos perfecte
i també creus impossible
que la seva ànima acusi
algun defecte.
             La llum l'abraça
i t'enlluerna i t'encén
l'oli del bronzejador
a la seva pell.

Anaxàgores va ser expulsat d'Atenes
acusat d'impietat per haver dit
que el sol només era una pedra incandescent.
Que cec que estava:
déu és tot allò que crema
i il·lumina.

AT THE BEACH

He's sunbathing with outstretched arms
on a brightly-coloured towel.
His fingers fiddle
with the sand.
              From where you're sitting
you can see his perfect body
and you also think how impossible
it is that his soul should reveal
any blemish.
              Light embraces him
and dazzles you and you're on fire
with the suntan oil
on his skin.

Anaxagoras was banished from Athens
accused of impiety for having said
that the sun was merely an incandescent stone.
How blind he was:
god is everything that burns
and gives light.

A L'AEROPORT

Seia en un banc de l'aeroport
a l'espera del seu vol,
no sé quin ni cap a on,
el món és tan ple de racons,
de ciutats on mai no faràs vida.

Per fer temps menjava una fruita
que els seus dits feien jugar
a la boca. I jo m'ho mirava
i hauria volgut ser-ne el pinyol
per com l'escurava,
per com el feia rodar amb cura
entre les dents.
Fins que va llançar-lo a la paperera
amb un gest indolent
i se'n va anar.

Hi ha històries d'amor tan breus
i vols tan llargs per lamentar-se'n.

AT THE AIRPORT

He was sitting on an airport bench
waiting for his flight,
I don't know which one or where it was going,
the world is so full of corners,
of cities where you'll never make a life.

To pass the time he was eating a piece of fruit,
his fingers and mouth toying
with it. And I was watching this
and wanted to be the stone
because of the way he scoured it,
the way he rolled it carefully
between his teeth.
Until with a lazy gesture
he threw it into the bin
and walked away.

There are love stories so brief
and flights so long you could weep.

SAURÍ

El vol erràtic d'uns ocells al vespre
et captiva. El missatge
que et transmeten, però,
ja no t'interessa.
Parlen de no sé què els harúspexs.
Allò que avancen els auguris,
ja no t'inquieta. I no t'importen
els enigmes dels oracles:
amb un somriure te'ls escoltes tots.
També els muts.

Abraçat a qui m'estimo,
sóc un saurí que ha trobat l'aigua
i llença les baquetes.

SEER

The wavering flight of birds at nightfall
captivates you. The message
they are bringing you, however,
is of no interest now.
The haruspices are muttering about something or other.
What the auguries portend
no longer worries you. And the oracles' enigmas
are now of no concern:
with a smile you listen to them all.
Even the mute ones.

Arms around the one I love,
I'm a dowser who has found water
and throws away his rods.

PER AMOR

L'edicte de l'emperador cristià així ho manava:
prohibit jugar a daus, explicar les lleis
i ensenyar filosofia. Havia d'emmudir,
d'un cop i per sempre,
l'Escola filosòfica d'Atenes.

Per amor a les idees
Damasci i els seus companys filòsofs
van decidir no renunciar als seus principis.
Per amor a les idees
van acordar exiliar-se.
A Pèrsia. I una petita comitiva
va travessar la xardor dels deserts de Síria,
el fang dels rius mesopotàmics,
les neus dels Zagres.
Per amor a les idees.

Què no fem per amor.

FOR LOVE

The edict of the Christian emperor decreed it thus:
it was forbidden to play at dice, to discuss the law
and to teach philosophy. He had to silence,
once and for all,
the Philosophy School in Athens.

For the love of ideas
Damascius and his fellow philosophers
decided not to renounce their principles.
For the love of ideas
they agreed to go into exile.
To Persia. And a little procession
made its way across the burning deserts of Syria,
across the mud of the Mesopotamian rivers,
the snow of the Zagres mountains.
For the love of ideas.

What will we not do for love.

IMATGES

Sec en un cafè davant el mar,
però s'esvaneix aquesta ciutat
i me n'apareix una altra:
allà on vam trobar-nos…
I se m'amunteguen les imatges.

Sant Joan Damascè té tres bells discursos
contra els iconoclastes
i sempre a favor de les imatges:
*El que és un llibre pels qui saben llegir,
és una imatge pels qui no llegeixen.
Allò que les paraules ensenyen per l'oïda,
una imatge ho fa pels ulls. Les imatges
són el catecisme dels qui no llegeixen.*

De tu l'únic que ara servo són imatges.
Les del goig. I tanco els ulls
per veure-les millor.
Els qui sabeu llegir
ja m'enteneu.

IMAGES

I sit in a café facing the sea,
but this town vanishes
and another one appears before me:
the one where we met…
and the images pile up before me.

St John of Damascus has three fine sayings
against iconoclasts
and always in favour of images:
What a book is for those who can read,
an image is for those who do not read.
What words teach through the ear,
an image teaches through the eyes. Images
are the catechism of those who cannot read.

All I have left of you now is images.
Images of pleasure. I shut my eyes
so as to see them better.
Those of you who can read
will understand me.

from
LLEI D'ESTRANGERIA / LAW GOVERNING ALIENS
(2008)

NOU MÓN

Cap crònica antiga no m'ha parlat mai de tu.
Ni del teu nom.
Ni del cos que m'has ofert
com un país amic
sense cap barrera a la frontera.
No m'ho anunciava cap oracle,
però has aparegut d'un nou món,
d'un demà que ahir no esperava.

Deleja tant la terra
que la vegin ulls de guaita.

L'amor és un port
que arriba per fi a un vaixell.

NEW WORLD

No ancient chronicle has ever mentioned you to me.
Not even your name.
Nor that body which you have offered me
like a friendly country
with no frontier barrier.
No oracle predicted it,
but you have appeared from a new world,
from a future which yesterday I didn't expect.

Land yearns so much
for watchful eyes to see it.

Love is a port
that finally comes to a ship.

CATACLISME

Vam estimar-nos sense edat.
Al capdavall, els dos
som de la mateixa era geològica,
i habitem uns paisatges
que abans foren de mamuts
i dinosaures. Nosaltres
també ens extingirem.
I el nostre amor, abans.
Com una espècie devorada per una altra
en un món primitiu
que es repetia en els gemecs
de l'un dins l'altre.

Que ràpid s'apagaren
els volcans dels nostres dies.
Seguí un temps lent de glaciació
i finalment l'adéu:
un meteorit impactà el nostre planeta
allunyant-lo
de la llum.

El teu nom ara,
fòssil de petxina
en un país sense mar.

CATACLYSM

We loved each other timelessly.
When all's said and done, we're both
from the same geological era,
and we inhabit landscapes
that previously held mammoths
and dinosaurs. We
too will become extinct.
And our love, sooner than that.
Like one species devoured by another
in a primitive world
repeating itself in the groans
of one inside another.

How swiftly they died out,
the volcanoes that were our days.
There followed a slow period of glaciation
and finally the farewell:
a meteorite struck our planet
pushing it away
from the light.

Your name now,
a fossilised shell
in a land without sea.

ISTANBUL

No sabia que un dia
et compararia a aquesta ciutat.
Tampoc que vindria sol a visitar-la
ni que t'escriuria aquesta carta
per dir-te
que quan fa fred en un país de calor,
penso en tu.
          Que quan al basar
venen fruita que no és de temporada,
penso en mi.
          Que quan algú paga més del compte
i l'estafen perquè no sap el canvi,
penso en nosaltres.

ISTANBUL

I didn't know that one day
I would compare you with this city.
Or that I would come to visit it on my own,
or that I would write you this letter
to tell you
that when it's cold in a hot country,
I think of you.
                    That when in the bazaar
they sell fruit that's out of season,
I think of me.
                    That when someone pays over the odds
and they swindle him because he's unfamiliar with the change,
I think of us.

LES PALMERES D'AL-FAIUM

… Sóc a l'oasi d'Al-Faium, a dues hores d'El Caire. Un amic meu té una casa enmig d'un palmerar i he vingut a passar-hi uns dies. La casa està encarada al llac Qarun, i quan et lleves, el primer que veus entre les flors a la finestra és l'aigua pintada de llum. Com l'únic ull d'un Ciclop que et mirés enamorat. Després el dia transcorre entre punyals de sol i carícies d'ombra dessota les palmeres o les parres. Jo vagarejo per les hortes i els vergers, passo el temps llegint, o bé al jardí de casa mig nu i descalç trenant mare-selves per adonar els meus futurs pecats mentre espero entre les hores els arabescs del cant dels muetzins. La tarda és un espectacle lent d'irisacions i de besllums fins que, de nit, farts del sopar i del vi, observem el cel negre per reconèixer-hi les formes dels cossos de nimfes o faunes que es convertiren en estrelles. Ahir, quan ja dormia, el meu amic em sacsejà fort al llit i em despertà: "Corre, vine, que veuràs una cosa!" I amb perplexitat em vaig alçar i vaig seguir-lo escales amunt fins al terrat. Era encara negra nit i de sobte feia molt de vent. Em va fer seure al pedrís davant l'estesa de palmeres que, amb el vent, batien els seus braços en totes les direccions i es despentinaven amb desordre. "Mira– va dir-me –el vent fa batre els beines de pol·len de les palmeres mascles i les palmeres femelles mouen així les fulles per recollir-lo i fecundar-se...Les palmeres estan fent l'amor." I vam quedar-nos la resta de la nit allà, batuts pel vent, en silenci, contemplant aquella escena.

THE PALM TREES OF AL-FAYOUM

… I 'm at the oasis of Al-Fayoum, two hours' drive from Cairo. A friend of mine has a house in the middle of a palm forest and I've come to spend a few days here. The house faces Lake Qaroun, and when you get up, the first thing you see through the flowers at the window is the water painted with light. As though the single eye of a Cyclops in love were looking at you. Thereafter the day passes, through daggers of sun and caresses of shade beneath the palms or climbing vines. I wander among the vegetable plots and the orchards, I spend the time reading, or in the garden beside the house barefoot and stripped to the waist weaving honeysuckle to adorn my future sins while I wait from hour to hour for the arabesques of song from the muezzins. The afternoon is a slow display of iridescence and diffused light until, with the coming of night, and full of supper and wine, we stare up at the sky in order to recognise the outlines of the bodies of nymphs and fauns who turned into stars. Yesterday, when I was already asleep, my friend shook me vigorously from my bed and woke me up: "Hurry, come along, and see something!" Mystified, I got up and followed him up the steps to the flat roof. It was still pitch black and suddenly very windy. He made me sit down on the stone bench in front of the expanse of palm trees which, with all that wind, were waving their arms in all directions, becoming tousled and dishevelled. "Look – he told me – the wind is beating the pollen sheaths on the male trees and the female trees are moving their leaves like this to gather it and become fertilised… The palm trees are making love." And we remained there the rest of the night, buffeted by the wind, not speaking, gazing at that scene.

MUSEU EGIPCI

Sala 27. Imperi mitjà.
La sang del cos que a la memòria s'ha fet pedra
torna a circular.
En la caricia a una estàtua
revisc el teu tacte:
tots els records bateguen
en aquest pit rosa de granit d'Assuan.

Quin estrany martell el temps,
que no esmica el desig.

Que inútil el rètol
"No tocar."

EGYPTIAN MUSEUM

Room 27. Middle Kingdom.
Blood in the body which in memory has turned to stone
begins to flow again.
Caressing a statue
I relive your touch:
all those memories are beating
in this rosy breast of Aswan granite.

What a strange hammer, time,
that never shatters desire.

How pointless the notice that says
"Do not touch."

from
CIÈNCIA EXACTA / EXACT SCIENCE
(2014)

NO ETS TU

No t'escarrassis a entendre
tot allò que dintre teu
retruny:
        són els records,
ciutats llunyanes, llum d'estius,
jungles que d'un dia per l'altre
han tornat erms, noms
i cossos amb què t'has barrejat,
delers que encara cremen,
somnis per complir,
passes fetes
en el fosc.

Que res de tot això no t'amoïni.
És com la roba que vesteixes cada dia:
té la teva forma
però no ets tu.

IT ISN'T YOU

Don't labour to understand
all the things rumbling away
inside you:
         they're memories,
distant cities, summer light,
jungles which, from one day to the next,
have become wilderness, names
and bodies with whom you've quarrelled,
desires that still smoulder,
dreams to be fulfilled,
steps taken
in the dark.

Let none of this disturb you.
It's like the clothing you wear every day:
it has your shape
but it isn't you.

PASSO EL TEMPS

Passo el temps cercant paraules
i el perdo entre silencis.
Per són allà, entre la por de dir
i la pena de callar,
pedres que intenten surar
en una fanguera.

Algú pla que riurà
davant aquest espectacle:
se m'eixorden les orelles
davant el paper en blanc.

I SPEND MY TIME

I spend my time searching for words
and waste it among silences.
But they're there, between the fear of speaking
and the pain of staying silent,
stones that try to float
in a muddy swamp.

Anyone seeing this sight
will roar with laughter:
my ears are deafened
by the blank page in front of me.

AQUELLA LLUM

Quan a poc a poc la penombra
ens vestia la nuesa, això
vas dir-me:
          que eres d'un vilatge
del Panjab, el país dels cinc rius,
tots tributaris del gran Indus.
Que a les seves ribes
homes i déus havien combatut.
Que la teva brunor de pell
era de la mescla d'indis
i de perses. Que els teus ancestres
també es remuntaven
als soldats grecs d'Alexandre.
Que el teu país l'havien governat
generacions de gurus
i d'endevins. Que el paisatge
era de prades immenses fins als Himàlaies.
Que als cims les neus eren perpètues.
Que a l'estiu eren miralls.
Que la llum,
          aquella llum…

– i jo la veia fulgurar als teus ulls,
immensa.

Sempre en el sol dels dies
recordo aquella nit.

THAT LIGHT

As twilight slowly
clothed our nakedness, this
is what you told me:
                    that you were from a village
in the Punjab, land of the five rivers,
all tributaries of the mighty Indus.
That on their banks
men and gods had fought.
That the brownness of your skin
was from the mix of Indian
and Persian. That your ancestors
went back as well
to the Greek soldiers of Alexander.
That your country had been ruled
by generations of gurus
and soothsayers. That the countryside
was made of vast meadows all the way to the Himalayas.
That on the summits the snows were everlasting.
That in summer they were mirrors.
That the light,
        that light…

– and I saw it flashing in your eyes,
immense.

In the days' bright sun
I remember that night.

ÈPOCA CLÀSSICA

Veneres els cossos de qui has estimat
com imatges de déus
que conservessin encara
algun poder. Miracles
ja no en fan, però ompliren
de meravelles i prodigis
els teus dies.

Ara són com bells quadres
d'una pinacoteca
que sala a sala
contemples lentament,
o una galeria d'estàtues
amb un gran rètol a l'entrada:
«Època clàssica».

I per tot el goig que fou,
ara els dediques aquests versos
agraït
com un captaire que torna
les monedes que li tiren.

THE CLASSICAL AGE

You worship the bodies of those you've loved
like images of gods
that might still retain some power. Miracles
they no longer perform, but they filled
your days with marvels
and with wonders.

They are now like beautiful paintings
in an art-gallery
that you gaze at slowly,
going from room to room,
or a museum full of statues
with a large sign at the entrance:
"The Classical Age".

And because of all the joy that there was,
you now dedicate these lines to them
in gratitude
like a beggar who gives back
the coins thrown down to him.

EN AQUELL BAR

El savi no cerca el plaer,
només l'absència de dolor.
                          Aristòtil

En aquell bar parlaves amb algú altre
una mica més enllà d'on jo seia.
I com es movia el vi dins la teva copa,
o eren els meus ulls
que vigilaven cada cop que mullaves
els teus llavis?

Ja no recordo jo què bevia,
copa o got, boca sense gust,
dolor.

Una arrel o un tubercle és el desig:
vol fer-se tija, fulles,
flor.

IN THAT BAR

> *The wise man does not seek pleasure,*
> *merely the absence of pain.*
>   ARISTOTLE

In that bar you were talking to someone else
a little beyond where I was sitting.
And how the wine moved in your glass,
or was it my eyes
keeping watch each time you moistened
your lips?

I don't remember what I was drinking,
from a glass or a tumbler, no taste in my mouth,
only pain.

Desire is a root or a tuber:
it wants to become stalk, leaves,
flower.

PASSO LA NIT

Passo la nit en clar
i recorro amb la pensa
la terra ara solitària
del que fórem.
              Una muntanya
penyalosa i elevada
la grimpo amb les mans
i amb els genolls.
Al cim: no res.
              Apesarat
i amb l'alè curt, contemplo
el paisatge desolat.
Tanta obaga.

Vaig aviar les meves ovelles
a péixer a casa el llop.

I SPEND THE NIGHT

I spend the night unable to sleep
and in my mind I go back over
the land, deserted now,
of what we were.
                        A mountain
high and full of crags
I climb on hands and knees.
On the summit: nothing.
                            Distressed
and out of breath, I stare down
at the desolate landscape.
All those hillsides the sun never touches.

I turned my sheep loose
to graze in the land of the wolf.

COM PLUJA ERRÀTICA

Com pluja erràtica,
de temps en temps
em véns a la memòria.

I què si va ser amb subterfugis,
amb arteries,
que al meu cos encès
hi vas tirar més llenya?

El vi glatia per sortir de l'ampolla,
anar ràpid de la copa
als llavis.
        Quants taps
van rodolar per terra?

I el record em fa somriure.
De temps en temps,
com pluja erràtica.

LIKE PASSING SHOWERS

Like passing showers
now and then
you come to mind.

And so what if it was through deceits,
through cunning ploys,
that you threw on my blazing body
yet more fuel?

The wine was yearning to spurt from the bottle,
to flow swiftly from glass
to lips.
 How many corks
rolled on to the floor?

And the memory makes me smile,
now and then,
like passing showers.

EL POEMA

Parlem només per vendre de nosaltres
requincalla. En la llacuna pantanosa
de tot el que diem,
gastem paraules
com vent que mou feixucs de joncs,
la canyavera.
              Però de sobte
un ànec alça el vol
i li brillen les plomes
de colors:
        el poema.

Escolteu el batre d'ales, contempleu-lo,
abaixades les escopetes
del silenci.

THE POEM

We talk merely to sell the ironmongery
of ourselves. In the marshy pool
of everything we say,
we waste words
like wind that moves the sluggish rushes,
the reed-bed.
         But suddenly
a duck takes flight
and its feathers gleam
with colours:
         the poem.

Listen to the beating of wings, gaze at it,
your shotguns of silence
lowered, for now.

BIOGRAPHICAL NOTES

MANUEL FORCANO has a PhD in Semitic Languages from the University of Barcelona. Having pursued Hebrew Studies in Israel, Arabic and Islamic Studies in Syria and Egypt, he lectured in Hebrew and Aramaic at the University of Barcelona (1996-2004). He has participated in the European Union MANUMED Project (2000-2004) to catalogue Arabic and Syriac manuscripts from countries on the southern rim of the Mediterranean, with active missions in Aleppo (Syria).

He has translated from Hebrew to Catalan the work of various modern Israeli poets such as Pinhas Sadeh, Ronny Someck and Yehuda Amichai, as well as the novel *The Same Sea* (2002) by Amos Oz. He has also translated Ibn Battuta's *Travels* (2005) from Arabic to Catalan, in conjunction with Margarida Castells. He published the book of historical and literary essays *The Crusades seen by the Jews* (2007), *History of Jewish Catalonia* (2010), *The Catalan Jews* (2014) and *50 Jewish sites in Catalonia* (2017). He has also translated and edited in Catalan the travels of Marco Polo, *The Description of the World* (2009), the cabalistic treatise *The Book of Creation* (2012), the legend of *The Golem* by Yudl Rosenberg (2013), and *The Jewish Anti-Gospels* (2017)

His own works of poetry include eight published books, noteworthy among which are *Corint* (2000), *Com un persa* (2001) (Like A Persian), winner of the 2002 Tivoli European Prize for best European poet under 36 years of age, *El tren de Bagdad* (2004) (The Baghdad Train), *Llei d'estrangeria* (2008) (Immigration Law), *Estàtues sense cap* (2013) (Headless Statues) and *Ciència exacta* (2014) (Exact Science).

Indebted to poets like K. Kavafis and Yehuda Amichai, the latter of whom he has translated, he frequently presents historical or cultural motifs from Antiquity, which contrast with the vulgarity of the present. A further contrast is between the pervasive erudition of his poems and his simplicity of tone and forms. Love and nostalgia for a glorious past are the two great themes in Forcano's poetry.

He has received many prizes for his poetic work.

He was the vice-President of the Catalan Council of Arts (2009-2011), the Manager Director of Private Foundation International Early Music Centre Jordi Savall (2004-2015), and Director of the Institut Ramon Llull for the international promotion of Catalan Language and Culture (2016-2018).

ANNA CROWE was born in Plymouth, and educated in France and Sussex. She studied French and Spanish at the University of St Andrews where she now lives, working as a writer and translator. She has also been a primary school teacher, taught at the former Bede Monastery Museum in Jarrow, and worked for many years in the Quarto, the much-missed second-hand bookshop. She has tutored for the Arvon Foundation, for the Open Association of St Andrews University, and for the Open College of the Arts, and led a poetry workshop for almost twenty years.

With others, in 1998 she founded StAnza, Scotland's Poetry Festival, was Artistic Director for the first seven years, and still serves as Honorary President on the Board of Trustees.

Her work includes two Peterloo collections, *Skating Out of the House* and *Punk with Dulcimer*, and three Mariscat chapbooks, *A Secret History of Rhubarb, Figure in a Landscape* (a PBS pamphlet Choice and winner of the Callum Macdonald Memorial Award) and *Finding My Grandparents in the Peloponnese*. She won the Peterloo Poetry Competition in 1993 and again in 1997, and has been a runner-up in the National Poetry Competition. She was awarded the Elmet Prize in 2018. Her work has been translated into Catalan, Spanish, German and Italian, including two of her collections: *Punk with Dulcimer* into Castilian by the Catalan poet, Joan Margarit, (Punk con salterio, Cosmopoética, 2008), and *Figure in a Landscape* into Catalan, (Paisatge amb figura, Ensiola, 2011), inspiring a series of lithographs by the

Mallorcan sculptor, Andreu Maimó; and into Spanish by the Mexican poet, Pedro Serrano, and published in Mexico as Figura en un paisaje (El oro de los tigres 2018).

Books of translation include an anthology of Catalan poems, *Light Off Water* (Miralls d'aigua), a joint Carcanet / Scottish Poetry Library publication; *Tugs in the Fog* (awarded a PBS Recommendation in 2006), *Strangely Happy* and *Love is a Place* by the Catalan poet, Joan Margarit, all published by Bloodaxe; the anthology *Six Catalan Poets, Peatlands*, selected poems by the Mexican poet, Pedro Serrano and *Lunarium*, poems by the Mallorcan poet, Josep Lluís Aguiló, all published in bilingual editions by Arc. Her third full poetry collection, *Not on the Side of the Gods*, is forthcoming from Arc in 2019.

In 2006 she received a Travelling Scholarship from the Society of Authors, to further her work of translation.

She lives in St Andrews with her partner, Dr Julian Crowe. They have three grown-up children and five grandchildren.